WORLD WAR II

HISTORY'S DEADLIEST CONFLICT

SIGNIFICANT BATTLES OF WORLD WAR II

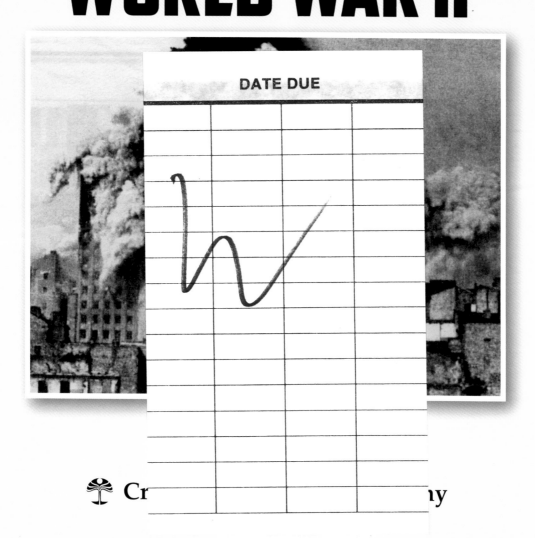

DATE DUE

🌳 Cr   ny

WORLD WAR II

HISTORY'S DEADLIEST CONFLICT

Author: Kelly Cochrane

Publishing plan research and development: Crabtree Publishing Company

Editors: Jackie Dell, Lynn Peppas

Proofreaders: Kelly Stern, Wendy Scavuzzo

Editorial services: Clarity Content Services

Production coordinator and prepress technician: Tammy McGarr

Print coordinator: Margaret Amy Salter

Series consultant: Fayaz Chagani

Cover design: Ken Wright

Design: David Montle

Photo Research: Linda Tanaka

Front cover: American fighter planes attacking a Japanese war ship in the Pacific Ocean

Title page: Bombing of Warsaw, Poland, August 1944

Table of contents: Soldiers of the 2nd SS Panzer Division and a Tiger I tank; The battleship USS Idaho fires at Japanese island of Okinawa on April 1, 1945; Enigma machine

Photo Credits:
Front cover: Thinkstock: © dudchik; Back cover: Wikimedia: public domain
Title page ww2today; p3 top Bundesarchiv, Bild 101III-Zschaeckel-206-35/Zschäckel, Friedrich/CC-BY-SA 3.0, US Navy/US Navy Naval History and Heritage Command/80-G-K-3829, wikipedia; p4 PD/German wikipedia; p5 top Bundesarchiv, Bild 183-C12701/CC-BY-SA, US Gov/American Battle Monuments Commission; p8 ww2today; p9 United Kingdom Government/Royal Navy; p10 IWM/A-3; p11 United Kingdom Government/IWM; p12 PD/United Kingdom/IWM ZZZ 3130C; p13 *MV Ardmore*, painting by Kenneth King, National Maritime Museum of Ireland/CC-BY-SA 1.0; p14 IWM/MH 4478; p15 US Gov/US War Dept.; p16 Tallandier/Bridgeman Images; p17 left US Gov/US War Dept./*Divide and Conquer (Why We Fight #3)*, The US National Archives and Records Administration/535713; p18 left PD/United Kingdom/IWM COL 188, PD/United Kingdom/IWM COL 186; p19 *A German attack on London in 1940 during World War II* (colour litho), Bond, William H. (20th Century)/National Geographic Creative/Bridgeman Images; p21 PD/United States of America; p22 US Gov; p23 Bundesarchiv Bild 146-1994-041-07/CC-BY-SA; p24 US Gov/US Army; p25 Sean Kilpatrick/The Canadian Press; p26 PD/United States of America; p27 frame from 1942 movie *Războiul nostru sfânt*/The National Archives of Romania; p29 PD/Poland; p30 top RIA Novosti Archive-324/Boris Kudoyarov/CC-BY-SA 3.0, ww2today; p31 Bundesarchiv, Bild 146-1992-055-33/Mährlen/CC-BY-SA; p32 top Karel Hájek/CC 3.0; p32 Bundesarchiv, Bild 101III-Zschaeckel-207-12/Zschäckel, Friedrich/CC-BY-SA; p34 Arthur Conry/CC 3.0; p35 ww2today; p36 wikipedia; p37 Bundesarchiv, Bild 101I-785-0287-08/CC-BY-SA; p38 PD/Poland; p39 US National Archives/USA C-5904; p40 US Gov/US Army/Center of Military History; p41 left Wikia/CC-BY-SA, ww2today; p42 US Gov/US Navy; p43 left US Navy/US Navy Naval History and Heritage Command/80-G-32367, US Gov/US Marine Corps; p44 left US Navy/US Navy Naval History and Heritage Command/80-G-K-3829, US Gov/US Army Signal Corps/US Naval Historical Center Photograph/SC 213700.

t=Top, bl=Bottom Left, br=Bottom Right

Library and Archives Canada Cataloguing in Publication

Cochrane, Kelly, author
　　Significant battles of World War II / Kelly Cochrane.

(World War II : history's deadliest conflict)
Includes index.
Issued in print and electronic formats.
ISBN 978-0-7787-2114-7 (bound).--
ISBN 978-0-7787-2118-5 (paperback).--
ISBN 978-1-4271-1696-3 (pdf).--ISBN 978-1-4271-1692-5 (html)

　　1. World War, 1939-1945--Campaigns--Juvenile literature. I. Title.

D743.7.C63 2015　　　　j940.54'1　　　　C2015-904378-6
　　　　　　　　　　　　　　　　　　　　　　　　C2015-904379-4

Library of Congress Cataloging-in-Publication Data

Cochrane, Kelly.
　　Significant battles of World War II / Kelly Cochrane.
　　　　pages cm. -- (World War II: history's deadliest conflict)
　　Includes index.
　　ISBN 978-0-7787-2114-7 (reinforced library binding) --
　　ISBN 978-0-7787-2118-5 (pbk.) --
　　ISBN 978-1-4271-1696-3 (electronic pdf) --
　　ISBN 978-1-4271-1692-5 (electronic html)
　　1. World War, 1939-1945--Campaigns--Juvenile literature. I. Title.

D743.7.C58 2015
940.54--dc23
　　　　　　　　　　　　　　　　　　　　2015023292

Crabtree Publishing Company

www.crabtreebooks.com　　1-800-387-7650

Printed in Canada/112015/EF20150911

Published in Canada
Crabtree Publishing
616 Welland Ave.
St. Catharines, Ontario
L2M 5V6

Published in the United States
Crabtree Publishing
PMB 59051
350 Fifth Avenue, 59th Floor
New York, New York 10118

Published in the United Kingdom
Crabtree Publishing
Maritime House
Basin Road North, Hove
BN41 1WR

Published in Australia
Crabtree Publishing
3 Charles Street
Coburg North
VIC, 3058

CONTENTS

THE CHANGING FACE OF WAR

In the early 1900s, the world was changing. The age of machines had arrived. Airplanes, automobiles, and other gas-powered vehicles were becoming common. This technology was changing not only society, but also how wars were fought.

War machines were bigger, faster, and more powerful than ever before. **Artillery** could fire more powerful missiles and shoot them farther. Planes were becoming faster and easier to control. The planes could also carry larger weapons. Airplanes launched from ships completely changed naval warfare. But air power was not the only change for the navies. New submarines meant that danger lurked below, too. War was becoming more dangerous and more destructive.

BELOW: *WWII brought huge advancements in technology and weaponry.*

LEFT: *For the German people, Hitler was the man who could lead them out of their misery and back to greatness.*

RIGHT: *The greatest tragedy of war is the loss of human life.*

WAR IS RARELY ABOUT GOOD AGAINST EVIL

Many of the ideas of the German leader Adolf Hitler were certainly evil. But it is wrong to look at the **Axis forces** as evil and the **Allied forces** as good. There were ordinary people on both sides of the conflict, and the circumstances of war demanded that people do things they would never have done outside of war. Perhaps the greatest evil was committed by both sides: the bombing of cities and the killing of **civilians**.

It is also a mistake to consider the Axis countries as the only group trying to expand their territory, power, and influence. The Allied countries were also fighting to protect and expand their influence in other parts of the world. For example, the British, Germans, and Italians fought for control of Egypt. Imagine what this battle looked like to Egyptians: three foreign countries fighting for control of their land.

World War II resulted in terrible destruction. Between 50 million and 70 million people died, almost half of them civilians. Countless buildings and homes were destroyed. The study of war should not be a study of good and evil, but of what should be avoided in the future.

Axis and Allied Territory, 1939

LEGEND
- Allied countries
- Allied-controlled
- Axis countries
- Axis-controlled
- USSR–Non-aggression agreement with Axis powers
- Neutral countries

THE WAR BEGINS

Germany, Italy, and Japan formed an alliance in the 1930s. This alliance is referred to as the Axis. At the end of August 1939, the USSR was not part of the Axis, but it had promised not to attack Germany. In 1939, Italy controlled Albania, and Germany controlled Austria and Czechoslovakia. Australia, Britain, Canada, France, and India—called Allied countries or the Allies—stood alone against the Axis.

Axis and Allied Territory, 1942

Iceland

N

Atlantic Ocean

LEGEND
- Neutral Nations in 1942
- Allied-controlled Areas in late-1942
- Axis-controlled Areas in late-1942

Norway

Finland

Sweden

Estonia

Soviet Union

Lithuania

Britain

Denmark

Latvia

Ireland

Netherlands

East Prussia

English Channel

Belgium

Germany

Poland

Czechoslovakia

Luxembourg

France

Austria

Hungary

Switzerland

Italy

Romania

Spain

Yugoslavia

Black Sea

Corsica

Bulgaria

Albania

Portugal

Sardinia

Greece

Turkey

Iran

Sicily

Cyprus

Syria

Iraq

Morocco

Tunisia

Lebanon

Algeria

Mediterranean Sea

Libya

Egypt

Saudi Arabia

USSR

Mongolia

Manchuria

China

Korea

Japan

Wake Is.

Iwo Jima

Burma

Okinawa

Siam

Formosa

Mariana islands

French Indo-China

Philippines

Guam

Malaya

Palau Is.

Marshall islands

Dutch East Indies

Caroline Islands

Gilbert islands

New Guinea

Australia

Solomon Islands

Guadalcanal

When the war began in 1939, Germany had only one **front** on which it focused its military might. That front was between Germany and the Allied countries to the west: the Western Front. By the middle of 1941, the Axis controlled almost all of mainland Europe. Hitler began his push east into the USSR, and south into the Mediterranean and North Africa. This opened two new fronts: the Eastern or Russian Front, and the Mediterranean Front and Africa. At the end of 1941, Japan attacked the United States, opening up conflict in the Pacific. At that time, the war truly became global.

CHAPTER 1

WWII BATTLES ON THE ATLANTIC OCEAN

Timeline

1939

December 13–17
Battle of the River Plate

July–October
First Happy Time

1941

May 24
Battle of Denmark Strait

1942

January–August
Second Happy Time

1943

May
Black May

The Battle of the Atlantic was the struggle to control the waters of the Atlantic Ocean. This was the longest battle of WWII, lasting almost the entire length of the war. It took place mainly in the north Atlantic as Germany attacked Allied supply ships moving between North America and Britain. But this battle was not fought just in the North Atlantic. For example, in 1942, Germany struck at ships all along the east coast of the United States and as far south as the Caribbean. The Allies had to win the Battle of the Atlantic because without supplies, Britain could not continue its war effort.

ALLIED NAVAL POWER

France and Britain had large, powerful navies. In 1939, Britain's Royal Navy was the strongest in the world. These Allied navies grew even stronger because they were joined by troops from Britain's **colonies**: Australia, Canada, India, and New Zealand. When the United States joined, the Allies became even more powerful. By the end of WWII, the U.S. Navy had added almost 1,200 major ships to its fleet. It was the largest navy in the world.

LEFT: *Canada played an important role in the Battle of the Atlantic. The Canadian **merchant ships** helped guard the **convoys** taking essential supplies across the North Atlantic. One out of every seven Canadian **merchant sailors** was either killed or wounded.*

RIGHT: *The danger of German U-boats was made clear early in the war. In the first six weeks, they sank the British aircraft carrier* Courageous, *the battleship* Royal Oak, *and more than 50 merchant vessels.*

Blockades

Just as they had done in WWI, the Allied forces used their naval power to set up **blockades**. All merchant ships entering the English Channel had to go into an Allied port to be searched. Allied ships patrolled the channel to make sure that rule was followed. Germany had a blockade strategy, too. It used its naval forces to sink as many military and supply ships as possible in the Atlantic Ocean before they could reach British ports. The naval forces also placed **sea mines** across the important shipping lanes.

THE AXIS NAVIES

The German navy, the *Kriegsmarine*, was small but modern. The Italian navy, the *Regia Marina*, was larger, but it did not have the latest technologies, such as **radar** or **sonar**. The Italian navy's involvement in the Atlantic was also limited because it was mainly active in the Mediterranean Sea.

Even though Germany's navy was small, it could have won the war if Grand Admiral Karl Doenitz had his way. Most military thinkers thought of sea warfare as large surface ships shooting at each other with cannons. It was for this reason that Hitler put so many of his resources into building large warships. But Doenitz wanted to shift this focus and build more U-boats. He believed that they were Germany's greatest naval weapon. In the end, Doenitz was proved right. Seven out of every ten Allied ships that were sunk in the war were sunk by U-boats. Many people believe that if Hitler had focused more on U-boats, Germany might have won the war.

SURFACE BATTLES

Surface battles were an amazing display of power. But large surface battle ships had little impact on the outcome of the Battle of the Atlantic. Even so, Allied victories at sea were important to **morale** because Germany appeared to be winning the war in the first few years of WWII.

The Battle of the River Plate

The battle began on December 13, 1939, in an area called the River Plate, near Argentina and Uruguay. A German ship called the *Graf Spee* attacked an Allied convoy that was being protected by three British warships. This attack led to the first major naval battle of WWII.

The British ships responded by attacking the *Graf Spee* from two sides. The German ship showed its power, damaging all three British ships and forcing them to retreat. But the *Graf Spee* was also heavily damaged and it headed into the port at Montevideo, Uruguay. Since Uruguay was a **neutral** country, the ship could not stay there. Rather than surrender his ship, the German captain ordered his crew to sink the *Graf Spee*.

Peru
Brazil
Bolivia
Uruguay
Paraguay
Chile
Argentina
Atlantic Ocean

Battle of the River Plate

HMS Cumberland leaves Falkland Islands

Falkland Islands

Parana River
Uruguay River
Uruguay
Juan L. Lacaze
Colonia del Sacramento
Buenos Aires
La Plata
Montevideo
Maldonado
Punta Piedras
Argentina
Bahia Samborombon
Atlantic Ocean
Punta Norte

Ajax Fires torpedoes
Graf Spee heads for Montevideo
Ajax: 2 turrets out of action
Graf Spee
Ajax and *Achilles* continue pursuit towards Montevideo
Exeter fires torpedoes
2 turrets out of action
Ajax
Exeter, heavily damaged, breaks off action
Achilles
fires torpedoes
Exeter
British cruisers sight *Graf Spee's* smoke
Exeter turns to engage
Atlantic Ocean

RIGHT: *In October 1940, the Allied convoy SC7 was attacked by a* **wolf pack**. *It lost 21 of its 30 ships. The convoy HX79, which was traveling close behind, lost 12 of its 49 ships.*

GERMAN U-BOATS: THE HAPPY TIME

German U-boats had so much success in the summer of 1940 that German submariners called this period the Happy Time. It was not a happy time for Allied sailors. Between June and October, German submarines sank 217 merchant ships, most of which were traveling alone.

At first, the German U-boats had success against single boats, but had less success against convoys. Most Allied ships traveled in convoys, so the Germans needed a strategy for attacking them.

Grand Admiral Doenitz ordered single U-boats to travel back and forth across a shipping lane and watch for a convoy. When a convoy was spotted,

> " The only thing that ever really frightened me during the war was the U-boat peril…our lifeline … was endangered. "
>
> —WINSTON CHURCHILL

the U-boat sent a message for other U-boats to meet it and attack as a group. The U-boats weaved through the convoy, attacked the ships, then fell back behind the convoy. **Escort** ships did not dare chase them because that would leave the convoy unprotected. A group of U-boats could follow a convoy for days, slowly wearing it down. This is similar to how wolves hunt, which is how these groups of U-boats got the name "wolf packs."

The Battle of Denmark Strait

On May 23, 1941, two German ships, the *Prinz Eugen* and the *Bismarck*, were spotted sailing through the Denmark Strait between Greenland and Iceland. The Germans claimed that the *Bismarck* was unsinkable. This was its first voyage and the Allies were waiting for it.

The British sent two of their most powerful battleships, the HMS *Hood* and the HMS *Prince of Wales*, toward the two German ships. On May 24, the British ships caught up with the German ships and opened fire. Only minutes into the fight, the *Hood* was ripped apart by a huge explosion. Fifteen minutes later, the *Prince of Wales* was forced to back off.

Angered by the loss of the *Hood*, the British navy hunted the *Bismarck* down. For two days, the ships played a cat-and-mouse game as the damaged *Bismarck* tried to escape. At one point the *Bismarck* appeared to have succeeded, but the *Bismark* was spotted by a British plane. On May 27, five British warships caught up with the *Bismarck* west of Brest, France. The German ship was pounded from

ABOVE: *Only 115 of the Bismarck's 2,222 crew members were saved. Some people claim that the Bismarck's crew tried to surrender during the battle but their surrender was ignored.*

both the air and the sea. After being struck with hundreds of shells and several **torpedoes**, the "unsinkable" *Bismarck* disappeared beneath the waves.

What do you think?
Why did the Allies think it was important to sink the *Bismarck*?

THE SECOND HAPPY TIME

When the United States entered the war in December 1941, many Americans still considered the war as something happening overseas. American ships sailed along the east coast as they always had, and coastal cities kept the lights on at night. This made the American ships easy targets for German U-boats lurking along the coast.

The Second Happy Time came in 1942. It started in January and continued until the fall of that year. During the summer of 1942, German U-boats sank 87 ships along the east coast of the United States. Some were sunk in full view of sunbathers on Miami Beach! Many people believe that if Hitler had sent more submarines into American waters, he might have changed the outcome of the war. They feel that the submarines could have damaged the U.S. Navy to the point where it would not have defeated Japan in the Pacific in the later years of the war.

RIGHT: *Despite the darkness, German U-boats off the east coast of the United States could see the outlines of American ships against the lights onshore. The ships were sitting ducks.*

THE END OF THE U-BOATS' REIGN OF TERROR

By 1943, wireless communications between Allied ships had become much better. This allowed convoys to avoid wolf packs and to develop strategies for chasing them off. The Allies had also built new air bases and aircraft that could fly longer distances. This allowed them to escort convoys farther. As a result, only 34 Allied ships were sunk in the Atlantic in May 1943, while 41 German U-boats were destroyed. German submariners called this month Black May.

The Allies also broke Germany's secret code. That meant the Allies knew where the German U-boats were positioned. After that, the U-boats were no longer the threat they once had been. This was a turning point in the Battle of the Atlantic. The Allies began to defeat the Axis more often.

CHAPTER 2

WWII IN EUROPE: WESTERN EUROPE

Timeline

1939

September 1–27
Invasion of Poland

1940

April 9–June 10
Invasion of Denmark
and Norway

May 10–June 22
Battle of France

July 10–October 31
Battle of Britain

1944–1945

June 6, 1944–May 1945
Battle for western
continental Europe

BELOW: *Much of Warsaw was reduced to rubble by German bombing. About 26,000 civilians died in the shelling.*

THE INVASION OF POLAND

Leading up to the beginning of World War II in September 1939, the Germans positioned more than one million troops along Poland's border. All Hitler needed was an excuse to attack. On August 31, a small group of German soldiers were ordered to dress in Polish uniforms and attack a German radio station near the Polish border. Hitler used this fake attack to claim that Poland had attacked first. On September 1, German warships opened fire on Polish ships in the Baltic Sea, and the *Luftwaffe* took to the air. (*Luftwaffe* was the official name for the German air force during WWII.)

The Soviets began invading Poland from the east on September 17. The Polish people fought back, but Germany and the Soviet Union defeated the Polish army. It took only seven days for the German army to reach the Polish capital, Warsaw. German troops captured Warsaw on September 27. Poland surrendered.

Poland was then divided between Germany and the Soviet Union. This was done according to an agreement between the two countries that was signed before the war.

RIGHT: *Never had the world seen a force as fast and powerful as the Panzer divisions.*

What Do You Know?

The Phony War

Britain and France declared war against Germany after it invaded Poland. The Polish army hoped that Britain and France would attack Germany from the west. But that attack never came. After rebuilding their own nations following WWI, Britain and France did not have the military strength to attack Germany. In fact, so little happened after the war was declared that some people called this time the Phony War.

BLITZKRIEG: LIGHTNING WAR

Before WWII, wars were fought by two armies facing each other in long lines. That was the way most military people thought of war. The German leadership imagined a type of warfare that was based on power and speed. This strategy became known as *blitzkrieg*, or lightning war.

When the Germans attacked Poland, they did it quickly. The German Air Force, the *Luftwaffe*, took control of the skies, and the German navy took control of sea ports. German planes destroyed enemy air defenses, bombed enemy positions, and dropped troops called paratroopers behind enemy lines.

On the ground, Panzer **divisions** punched through the enemy lines. These fighting units consisted of fast-moving armored vehicles, such as tanks, for carrying soldiers and artillery. The Panzer divisions broke up the enemy lines. The German infantry, or foot soldiers, then followed and destroyed the small pockets of enemy soldiers.

What do you think?
Why do you think the *Luftwaffe* bombed bridges, roads, and railways? What effect did that have?

LEFT: *The German force that moved through the Ardennes region was massive. The line of artillery, tanks, vehicles, and men stretched for almost 100 miles (161 km).*

HITLER LOOKS WEST

Even before the mission in Poland was over, Hitler was planning his move into France. Much of France's military was focused on creating a strong line of **fortification** along the French–German border. This line of defense was called the Maginot Line, and the French believed it could not be broken.

With the Maginot Line protecting its eastern border, France sent forces north into Belgium to stop the Germans who were approaching Belgium from the east. The French were joined by 150,000 British troops called the British Expeditionary Force (BEF). But Hitler moved another large force into the Ardennes region. This region was between the Maginot Line and the Allied forces to the north.

The Allies had stationed a few troops there because they thought it was impossible for an armored division to travel through the hilly, heavily forested area. They were wrong.

A total of 45 German divisions passed through the Ardennes over a matter of weeks. They easily defeated the French forces, then pushed farther west. The Germans had the Allies surrounded on three sides. The Allies were forced to fall back until they reached the sea at Dunkirk. They were trapped.

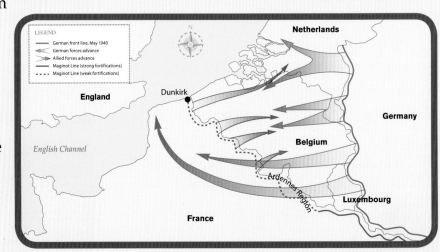

The Dunkirk Miracle

If Hitler had allowed his army to move forward, the Allied forces at Dunkirk would have been crushed. But he ordered his army to wait for three days before making a final assault. It is uncertain why Hitler did this. One theory is that he wanted his army to catch up to the armored units to create a force so large that it could not fail. Whatever the reason was, his decision was a mistake. While the Germans waited, the Allies acted. Between May 26 and June 4, 1940, 340,000 British and French soldiers were **ferried** across the English Channel to safety. Hitler had let the enemy escape.

ABOVE: *Hundreds of British military and civilian ships crossed the English Channel to rescue the Allied soldiers trapped at Dunkirk.*

What do you think?
Why do you think it was such a big mistake for Hitler to have allowed the Allied soldiers to escape at Dunkirk?

THE BATTLE OF FRANCE

While the armies at Dunkirk had been saved, France had not. The German Army marched south toward Paris. British, Canadian, and French forces fought back, but could not stop the German forces. The situation was made worse on June 10, 1940, when Italy joined the war on the German side.

To protect Paris from being destroyed, the French government declared it an open city. This meant it would be left undefended, and enemy troops could enter without **resistance**. On June 14, 1940, German troops marched into Paris and raised the **Nazi** flag on top of the Eiffel Tower. Eight days later, on June 22, the French surrendered. Britain, Australia, Canada, New Zealand, and South Africa were left to fight Germany.

ABOVE: *The Luftwaffe bombed Paris on June 3, killing more than 200 civilians. Many people question why the Germans did this, considering that their victory was already assured.*

THE BATTLE OF BRITAIN

Only weeks after France fell, the Germans began Operation Sea Lion—their plan to invade Britain. Germany planned to move 260,000 troops by ship across the English Channel into southern England. The German navy and air force bombed ships and ports along the English coast to prepare for German troops to move across the channel. This was the start of the Battle of Britain.

The *Luftwaffe* Falls Short

For Operation Sea Lion to succeed, Germany had to control the skies. The head of the *Luftwaffe*, Hermann Goering, told Hitler that controlling the skies would not be a problem. He believed he could clear the skies of the British Royal Air Force (RAF) within four weeks. But Goering was mistaken. Although the *Luftwaffe* was a much larger force than the RAF, only two thirds of its planes were within **striking range** of Britain. Goering also did not realize how many fighter planes the RAF had. One other advantage the RAF had was that the air battle took place over British soil. If British planes were in trouble, they could land and be rescued. German planes that were in trouble could not land, so the planes and their pilots were captured or destroyed.

BELOW: *The British fighter planes, called Spitfires and Hurricanes, were effective against German planes. Britain had built a sophisticated early-warning system that included the use of radar. This helped give Britain an advantage over the Germans, who had not pursued radar development aggressively.*

RIGHT: *German planes accidently bombed London in late August 1940. The German pilots mistook the night lights of London for their targets at British airbases and airfields.*

A MISTAKE THAT CHANGED HISTORY

Between July and October 1940, German planes bombed targets inside Britain. At first, they targeted British airbases and airfields. The RAF defended the British skies, but by mid-August 1940, RAF was exhausted. It could not continue much longer.

On August 24, everything changed. A group of German bombers got lost on the way to their targets. When they saw lights below them, they dropped their bombs and returned to base. But the lights they had seen were not those of their targets, they were the lights of London. The German bombers had accidentally bombed the British capital.

The bombing of London was the excuse that British prime minister Winston Churchill was looking for to attack German cities. The next night British bombers were ordered to strike the German capital, Berlin. The city was bombed five more times over 11 days.

Hitler was furious. He ordered the *Luftwaffe* to move its focus from the RAF airfields to British cities. London was its main target. This gave the RAF a chance to repair airplanes and runways, train pilots, and regain its strength. Even though daily bombings of Britain continued, it was clear by October that Hitler had lost the Battle of Britain. Operation Sea Lion would never happen.

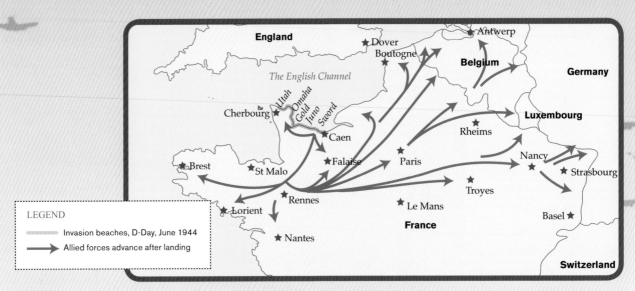

ABOVE: *By the end of June 1944, 850,000 troops, 150,000 vehicles, and almost 600,000 tons of supplies had crossed into France from Britain. British and Canadian forces then moved south and east. American troops moved into western France and Brittany.*

THE TIDE TURNS ON GERMANY

The Allies developed a plan called Operation Overlord to defeat Germany. It involved sending troops to Normandy, France. On the night of June 6, 1944, a massive Allied force set off across the English Channel from England. Almost 7,000 ships carried more than 131,000 British, Canadian, and American troops. June 6, the day of the Allied **offensive,** is often referred to as D-Day.

The Allied troops landed at five Normandy beaches, code-named Utah, Omaha, Gold, Juno, and Sword. The British troops landed at Gold and Sword beaches; the American troops landed at Utah and Omaha beaches; and the Canadian troops landed at Juno Beach. Before the troops reached the French shores, British and American bombers and warships **bombarded** the French coastline. At the same time, British and American paratroopers dropped near the beaches. By the end of the day, the Allies had the **foothold** they needed in France. But the human

What Do You Know?
Sacrifices at Dieppe
The Allies had tried to invade France two years before D-Day. On August 19, 1942, 6,100 soldiers attempted to land at Dieppe, France. About 5,000 of those troops were Canadians. The attack force was not large, so it depended on surprise. Unfortunately, the ships carrying the troops were spotted and attacked by a small German convoy. That alerted the German land forces. The Allied troops landed at five places along the coast, but were met with heavy resistance and had to retreat. The Allied losses were heavy.

cost was devastating. When the Battle of Normandy was over, more than 425,000 Allied and German soldiers were missing, wounded, or dead.

THE BATTLE OF BRITTANY

After gaining control of the Normandy beaches, most Allied forces moved south and east. But the Americans were given the task of clearing the German forces from Brittany, a province in northwestern France.

What do you think?

Why do you think controlling the ports in France was so important to both the Germans and the Allies?

They were also ordered to capture the ports at St-Malo, Brest, Lorient, and Saint-Nazaire.

The German forces drew back into the port cities. Hitler had told his commanders to defend them "to the last man and the last bullet." It took more than one week of heavy shelling and street-fighting before the Americans captured St-Malo. Brest did not fall until September 18. The Allies decided that the cost of taking the ports was too high. They decided to surround Lorient and Saint-Nazaire so that the Germans could not use the ports or make an escape. The cities stayed under German control until the end of the war.

BELOW: *Great historical buildings and works of art were destroyed in many towns and cities throughout Europe. The historic towns of St-Malo and Brest were also destroyed.*

THE BATTLE OF ARNHEM

As the Allies moved east, getting supplies to the front line was becoming more difficult. Many believed that things would get worse as winter came. British Field Marshal Bernard Montgomery suggested a plan called Operation Market Garden. This plan involved capturing bridges near the **Dutch** city of Arnhem and entering Germany from the north. He believed this plan would end the war by Christmas.

Operation Market Garden involved the largest drop of paratroopers ever attempted—more than 10,000. The plan began on September 17, 1944. However, it quickly started to fall apart. Allied troops were not able to move fast enough, and the German force at Arnhem was too large. Montgomery's plan for a two-day mission instead lasted ten days. In the end, the bridge at Arnhem was not captured. Even worse, only about 2,000 of the 10,000 Allied soldiers involved in the fighting returned home. Arnhem was eventually **liberated** after a series of battles fought by British, Canadian, and American troops. Those troops pushed the German troops out of the country.

More than 10,000 Allied paratroopers were dropped around Arnhem. Many of those men died because the Germans had learned the location of the drop and attacked the men in the air.

THE BATTLE OF THE BULGE

By December 1944, Hitler was desperate. There were about 83,000 Allied troops close to his western border, with thousands more not far behind. He positioned along his border a German force of 275,000 soldiers, 1,900 artillery, 1,000 armored vehicles, and 1,000 planes. He hoped to push through and capture the Belgian port of Antwerp. This city was the Allies' main source of supplies.

The German operation started off well, but soon ran into strong Allied resistance. The result was more of a bulge in the Allied defenses, not a break. The American and British troops attacked the German forces from the north and south. By January 16, the German offensive was defeated. It lost 100,000 men and most of its tanks and aircraft.

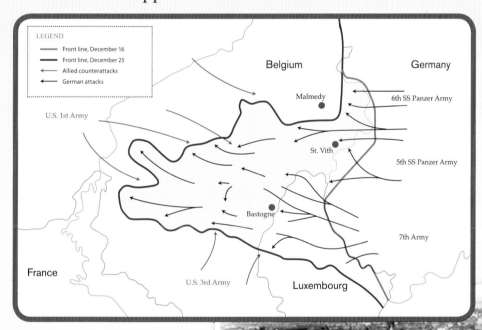

LEGEND
— Front line, December 16
— Front line, December 25
← Allied counterattacks
← German attacks

Belgium

Germany

Malmedy

6th SS Panzer Army

U.S. 1st Army

St. Vith

5th SS Panzer Army

Bastogne

7th Army

France

U.S. 3rd Army

Luxembourg

LEFT: *The Germans pushed the Allied front lines back, but the Allies moved their defenses into position in front of the German force.*

RIGHT: *In February 1945, the Allies bombed the German city of Dresden over the course of two nights. The bombs exploded into huge fireballs, killing more than 20,000 civilians and destroying many of the buildings.*

THE BATTLE FOR GERMANY

The Rhine River was the last natural **obstacle** the Allies needed to overcome before moving into Germany's **heartland**. A force made up of British, Canadian, and American troops crossed the river in the north near Düsseldorf. Other American troops crossed near Cologne and Mannheim. By March 25, 1945, the Allies controlled all the territory to the west of the Rhine and had moved 28 miles (45 km) east of the river.

What Do You Know?

Hitler ordered all the bridges over the Rhine to be destroyed. The Ludendorff Bridge near Remagen was wired with explosives. While American soldiers rushed onto the bridge, German engineers tried to set off the explosives. Some detonated, but the main **charge** did not blow. Machine-gun fire rained down on the American soldiers as they ran from one support beam to the next. The German troops were unable to stop the Allies, and by the end of the day, the Ludendorff Bridge was in Allied hands. Over the next week, more than 25,000 Allied troops and tons of supplies and vehicles crossed the bridge.

> " While we were running across the bridge ... I spotted this lieutenant standing out there completely exposed to the machine-gun fire .... cutting wires and kicking the German demolition charges off the bridge with his feet! "
>
> —SGT. ALEXANDER A. DRABIK, THE FIRST AMERICAN SOLDIER TO CROSS THE LUDENDORFF BRIDGE

RIGHT: *The Germans continued to attack the Ludendorff Bridge near Remagen. On March 17, it finally collapsed with more than 100 combat engineers on it. Twenty-four Allied soldiers were killed.*

THE ALLIES CAPTURE BERLIN

Even though Germany had signed a peace pact with the Soviet Union at the beginning of World War II, the Germans still attacked the Soviets. This act of aggression caused the Soviets to join the Allies. From 1941 to 1945, the Soviets fought the Germans alone on the Eastern Front. Soviet soldiers captured Berlin on May 2, 1945. The Battle of Berlin caused great destruction of the city and tens of thousands of soldiers from both sides lost their lives.

While Soviet troops pushed westward in 1945, Canadian and British troops took control of northern Germany. They blocked German troops from moving south from Norway and Denmark to help defend Berlin. Canadian troops also moved into Netherlands. American troops pushed into central and southern Germany, as far as the Elbe River. They surrounded the Ruhr Valley, which was Hitler's main source for coal and steel. Some German troops fought back, while others simply surrendered. The American troops took more than 325,000 prisoners. The war with Germany was almost at an end.

BELOW: *After the battle at Arnhem, Germany blocked all food and fuel from reaching **Holland**. More than 22,000 Dutch citizens died from starvation. The Canadians liberated Holland and are regarded as heroes to this day.*

CHAPTER 3

WWII IN EUROPE: EASTERN EUROPE

Timeline

1939

August 23
Germany and the Soviet Union sign the Molotov–Ribbentrop Pact

1939–1940

November 30, 1939– March 13, 1940
The Soviet Union invades Finland (the Winter War)

1941–1945

June 1941–May 1945
Battle for Soviet Union

Hitler faced a **dilemma** even before the war began. If he invaded Poland, Britain and France would declare war against Germany. Hitler was willing to risk that, but he could not risk being at war with Britain and France on the Western Front and with the Soviet Union on the Eastern Front. That would split his forces.

The Soviet leader Joseph Stalin knew war was coming. He also knew that his army was not strong enough to stand up to the Germans. He was in talks with Britain about possibly forming a partnership, or an alliance. But on August 23, 1939, the Soviets shocked the world by signing an agreement with the Germans that said neither side would attack the other for at least ten years. This agreement was called the Molotov– Ribbentrop Pact and was often referred to as a non-aggression pact.

With the signing of this non-aggression pact, Hitler did not have to worry about the Soviets attacking him on the Eastern Front.

LEFT: *Joachim von Ribbentrop, on the right, represented Germany in the discussions leading to the non-agression pact. Vyacheslav Molotov, on the left, was the Soviet representative.*

RIGHT: *The Soviets took over some Baltic states, including Bessarabia and Bukovina in Romania. Citizens were forced to leave their homes.*

THE SOVIET UNION INVADES FINLAND

Stalin knew Hitler wanted to expand Germany's borders to the east, and that the Soviet army would have to face the Germans one day. He planned to build up his military during the 1930s. He also planned to capture lands in neighboring countries. These lands would create a separation, or buffer, between the Soviet Union and Germany.

The first buffer Stalin wanted to create was in eastern Finland. He planned to place troops there to defend against an attack that might come through Scandinavia. He also wanted to control shipping through the Gulf of Finland. But Finland refused to give up control of any of its land or ports. So on November 30, 1939, Stalin's Red Army invaded.

The Soviet Army Gets a Surprise

The Soviets didn't expect the war for Finland to last long. The Finnish army only had about 33,000 troops and lacked modern equipment. But they knew the **terrain** better, and they were more prepared for winter warfare. It took three months before both sides agreed to negotiate. The Soviets got what they wanted, but lost more than 200,000 troops and hundreds of tanks, airplanes, and artillery in the process.

HITLER BREAKS HIS PROMISE

In 1941, Stalin was warned that Germany was gathering troops on his western border. But Stalin refused to believe that Hitler would break the Molotov–Ribbentrop Pact. On June 22, 1941, Hitler proved him wrong, launching Operation Barbarossa—the surprise invasion of the Soviet Union.

Operation Barbarossa was the largest military operation ever put together. The *Luftwaffe* started the attack, destroying Soviet airfields and aircraft. It quickly destroyed more than 1,200 Soviet planes and by the end of the first day, Germany controlled the skies. At the same time, thousands of German artillery shelled Soviet positions. German Panzer divisions crashed through Soviet lines, cutting deep into Soviet territory. About three and a half million German troops pushed eastward into the USSR.

What Do You Know?

Hitler's Plans for the Soviet Union

Hitler wanted to use the lands east of Germany as *lebensraum*, or "living space," for the German people. He planned to force the Soviet people into **Siberia** and replace them with Germans. Slavs (people mostly from Eastern Europe) were to be used for slave labor, and Jewish people would be killed.

LEGEND
- ▪▪▪ German forces start line, June 1941
- ⋯⋯ Front line, September 1941
- → German forces advance

LEFT: *There were three prongs to Germany's attack on the Soviet Union: one toward Leningrad in northern Russia; one toward Moscow in central Russia; and one toward Kiev in Ukraine, just south of Russia. In pushing south, Germany hoped to also capture the Ukrainian port of Odessa.*

CIRCLES OF DESTRUCTION

Germany's divisions cut through Soviet lines, quickly capturing Soviet territory. The divisions would encircle, or surround, Soviet troops or cities. They would then either attack the trapped people or lay siege to them, which means that all supplies would be blocked from reaching the people.

Encircling Soviet Troops at Kiev

During the Battle of Kiev, the Germans captured more than 650,000 Soviet troops. This was the largest military encirclement in history. But this victory cost Hitler dearly. To surround Kiev, Hitler had borrowed large numbers of troops from the armies moving toward Moscow. This choice delayed the attack on Moscow by about one month. This delay may have lost the Germans the ability to capture Moscow. It may even have cost them the war.

What do you think?
Explain why a siege would be effective. What effect would a siege have on the people of a city?

BELOW: *About two million Soviet soldiers died after they were captured by the Germans. Some were executed, and many died in camps surrounded by barbed wire, with no shelter and little food.*

THE SIEGE OF LENINGRAD

Few events show the hardships and cruelty of war more than the siege of Leningrad (now called St. Petersburg). The German attack on the city failed, so the Germans laid siege to it. After September 8, 1941, the Germans blocked all supplies from reaching the city. Hitler then ordered that the city be bombed to dust. The civilian population of Leningrad suffered terribly.

The Soviet people quickly ran out of heating fuel. The pipes in unheated buildings froze and burst, so homes had no electricity, heat, or water. Food was also scarce. The government gave **rations**, but the rations were small. Every animal in the city was eaten, including the rats. The main source of nourishment was bread made from flour, wood shavings, and sawdust.

> " My Ninochka cried all the time, long and drawn out, and she couldn't go to sleep. [I had no milk] … so I [cut my arm and] gave her my blood to suck… "
>
> —SOVIET MOTHER DURING THE SIEGE OF LENINGRAD

LEFT: *The siege of Leningrad ended on January 27, 1944, when German troops withdrew. At least 670,000 of Leningrad's citizens died, most by starvation.*

BELOW: *Some supplies made it to Leningrad across ice roads on Lake Ladoga. But this route was only open in the winter.*

RIGHT: *Thousands of German soldiers could not fight because of frostbite. Many froze to death.*

THE BATTLES FOR MOSCOW AND STALINGRAD

Germany's plan was to capture the Soviet capital, Moscow. But the German advancement was delayed when Hitler moved some of the troops to Kiev and Stalingrad (now called Volgograd). By October 1941, the focus was back on Moscow.

Moscow's Greatest Ally: Winter

Hitler did not equip his forces for a winter war. He thought the Soviets would fall before Christmas. But he had underestimated the Soviet army. That mistake and the Germans' delay meant that the battle took longer than expected.

It became difficult for the Germans to get supplies to their armies. As Soviet soldiers retreated from the Germans, they were given orders to destroy anything of value. This was known as Stalin's "scorched-earth" policy. The war in the Soviet Union was becoming a war of attrition, which is a strategy in which a country slowly chips away at its enemy's resources and wears it down. Stalin was able to get more food, weapons, vehicles, and troops. However, the Germans were not able to replenish their supplies.

In December 1941, weakened German troops got close to Moscow, but the Soviets began to push back. By January, the Germans were 150 miles (240 km) from Moscow, and any hope of capturing the capital was gone.

Failure at Stalingrad

With the dream of capturing Moscow lost, Hitler increased his efforts in Stalingrad. He ordered the city to be burned down. Stalin sent more than 250,000 troops to surround the city. About 100,000 Germans were trapped and had to surrender. Only about 5,000 of these prisoners made it out of the Soviet Union alive.

The German loss at Stalingrad was a turning point of the war. The Soviets continued to push the weakened German forces back. The goal was to push them back into Germany and to take back Berlin.

> " Ask any soldier what half an hour of hand-to-hand struggle means in such a fight. And imagine Stalingrad: eighty days and eighty nights of hand-to-hand struggles... Stalingrad [was] no longer a town. "
>
> —DIARY OF LIEUTENANT WEINER OF THE 24TH PANZER DIVISION

RIGHT: *The Germans' last offensive against the Soviets was at Kursk in southwestern Russia between July 5 and August 23, 1943. It was the largest tank battle in history.*

THE PUSH TO BERLIN

Hitler rushed 800,000 troops to the Eastern Front in hopes of stopping the Soviet **advance**. But by April 20, 1945, Soviet troops were on the outskirts of Berlin. The battle for Berlin lasted 12 days. Hilter knew he would be defeated, so he committed suicide on April 30. On May 2, the Germans surrendered the city. One week later, on May 8, the Allies declared victory in Europe.

BELOW: *Fighting continued in Czechoslovakia. The battle for Prague, called the Prague Offensive, started on May 6, 1945, and did not end until the Soviets took control on May 11.*

CHAPTER 4

WWII IN THE BALKANS, THE MIDDLE EAST, THE MEDITERRANEAN, AND AFRICA

Timeline

1940–1941

October 1940–June 1941
Battle of the Balkans

August 1940–May 1941
Battle for East Africa

1940–1943

September 1940–May 1943
Battle for North Africa

1943

July–September
Battle for Italy

1944

January–May
Battles of Monte Cassino

The **Balkan Peninsula** is in southeastern Europe. In 1939, this region included parts of Albania, Bulgaria, Greece, Yugoslavia, and Turkey. Germany had a good relationship with Bulgaria, Hungary, Romania, and parts of Yugoslavia. Albania was controlled by Germany's **ally** Italy. Greece had a relationship with Britain, but was neutral.

Hitler wanted the Balkans to stay at peace. Once he finished in France and Britain, he planned to move into the Soviet Union. If fighting broke out to the south, his plans would be difficult to carry out.

On October 28, 1940, Italian **dictator** Benito Mussolini invaded Greece. But the Greek army pushed the Italians back and took over part of Albania. Of even greater concern for Hitler was that on March 5, 1941, Britain sent troops to Greece to assist in its fight against Italy. That meant Britain had a foothold on the continent. It might use this position to launch attacks on Germany from the south.

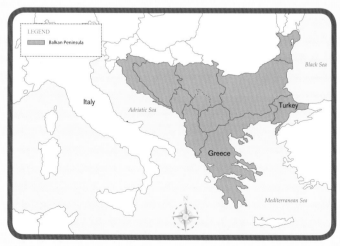

LEFT: *The Balkan region in 1939.*

THE INVASION OF GREECE

Hitler needed to bring Greece under Axis control and force Britain off the continent. He made agreements with Bulgaria, Hungary, and Romania, bringing them into the Axis. This allowed him to place troops along the Greek border. To complete his control of the territory north of Greece, Hitler also needed to control Yugoslavia.

Much of Yugoslavia's population supported Germany. But in late March 1941, its government was taken over by British supporters. Hitler responded by attacking the Yugoslavian capital, Belgrade. For two days, bombs rained down on the city. German, Italian, and Hungarian troops then attacked on the ground. Just 12 days later, on April 17, Germany was in control of Yugoslavia. Once Hitler controlled the lands to the north of Greece, he turned his attention south. On April 6, 1941, German troops crossed into Greece through Bulgaria. The Greek and Allied forces attempted to fight off the attack, but were forced to retreat south. The Allied forces escaped the Greek mainland, fleeing to the Greek island of Crete and to North Africa. On April 24, 1941, Greece surrendered.

German Soldiers Fall from the Crete Skies

Hitler could not leave Crete as a base for the Allies. On May 20, 1941, the Germans struck the island with a massive bombing raid, followed by thousands of paratroopers. By June, Crete had fallen to Germany and the Allies had lost their foothold in southern Europe.

RIGHT: *Germany lost 220 of the 500 aircraft that dropped paratroopers into Crete. A large number of the paratroopers were killed before they hit the ground.*

WAR IN AFRICA AND THE MIDDLE EAST

The Middle East includes countries in southwest Asia and northeast Africa. This region has rich resources, including oil fields. The Allied force was afraid that the Axis would take control of this region and its resources. The British military was also worried that the Axis could launch attacks on British-controlled territories from there.

Italian Attacks in East Africa

Italy already controlled areas in East Africa. But Mussolini wanted to have more influence. On August 3, 1940, he sent forces into British-controlled areas of Somaliland, which included the British port at Berbera. Italian forces attacked small areas inside the borders of Sudan and Kenya. By August 19, Italy controlled these areas.

The British did not want the Axis to gain areas south of Egypt or along the important shipping routes in the Red Sea. Soldiers from British colonies, such as Australia, Canada, and India, pushed back. In some places, such as the southern town of Keren in Eritrea, the fighting was fierce. In other places, the Italians left the battlefields without surrendering to the Allied forces. By May 1941, the British had taken control of East Africa away from Italy.

BELOW: *It took the British three tries to capture the town of Keren, during February and March 1941. The terrain made the journey to the city very difficult.*

THE SEESAW BATTLE FOR NORTH AFRICA

If the Axis won control of Egypt, it would have control of the Suez Canal, an important trade route for all nations.

In September 1940, the Italian army moved into Egypt. The British only had about 35,000 troops stationed there. After four days, however, the Italians stopped due to supply problems.

Britain's Secret Weapon

The Italians had supply problems because the Royal Navy had attacked and sunk more than half of their supply ships that were trying to get to the North African coast. The Allies' plan was successful due to the information-gathering program. The Allies were listening to Axis communication and learned when and where troops and supplies were being moved.

The Italian force in the desert quickly weakened due to the lack of food and fuel. The British attacked and managed to push the Italians out of Egypt. By December 1940, they had also captured the Libyan territory, including the important port of Tobruk.

RIGHT: *An ENIGMA machine*

What Do You Know?

Allied commanders received valuable information from a spy named Boniface throughout the war. The information was code-named ULTRA. But there was no Boniface. The ultra-secret information was actually coming directly from the Germans!

The Germans sent coded messages through a machine called ENIGMA. They believed the ENIGMA code was unbreakable. But Allied mathematicians broke the code early in the war. The Allies secretly listened to German communications, and passed the information on to their commanders. Boniface was made up to hide the fact that the code was broken. The secret was not revealed until 30 years after the war!

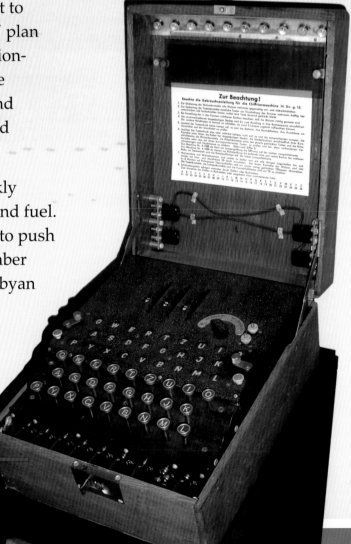

Germany Responds

To support the Italians, Hitler sent a German fighting unit called the *Afrika Korps*, led by General Erwin Rommel. By April 1941, the *Afrika Korps* had pushed the British out of Libya and into Egypt. Rommel could not take the Libyan port of Tobruk, so he laid siege to it.

Rommel captured Tobruk in 1942, after defeating the Allies in the Battle of Gazala. When the British lost the port, the United States agreed to help them in North Africa. America's firepower tipped the seesaw in the Allies' favor. In the coming months, the Axis forces were pushed back into Tunisia. In May 1943, more than 230,000 Axis troops surrendered. The battle for North Africa was over.

ABOVE: *On June 21, 1942, General Rommel captured the port of Tobruk in Libya and a large number of troops, supplies, and Allied tanks.*

Battles of El Alamein

El Alamein, Egypt, was the site of two major British victories in 1942. The first was in July, when Allied forces stopped Rommel's attack on Egypt. The second came between October 23 and November 4 when the British were on the attack. Rommel's forces were dug in at El Alamein, threatening British control of Egypt. They also stopped the British from pushing into Libya. The Allied forces broke through Rommel's lines, forcing the Germans to start the retreat that would end in Tunisia.

WAR IN ITALY

Now that the Allies controlled North Africa, they could focus on regaining southern Europe. On July 9, 1943, Allied ships moved toward Sicily. Paratroopers dropped into Sicily, but they were scattered by strong winds. By July 10, the American, British, and Canadian troops held about 75 miles (120 km) of the south Sicilian coast.

British and Canadian forces fought their way east, while the Americans headed north and west. Fighting was fierce in some places, while in other places the troops won easily. The heat and rough terrain made moving the troops very difficult. But by August 17, the Allied forces had fought their way through the enemy and met at Messina, on the northeastern tip of the island. The Allies had control of Sicily.

ITALY SURRENDERS

Before the Allies reached Messina, Mussolini had been removed from government and was put in prison. The Italian government surrendered to the Allies on September 3, 1943. Even though Italy was out of the war, Germany and the Allies continued to fight for control of the country. Over the next two years, more than 100,000 Axis and Allied troops lost their lives in Italy.

LEFT: *To reach Rome, the Allies had to get past a hill called Monte Cassino. Between January 17 and May 18, 1944, the Allies and Germans fought four battles there. The Allies won, but the battles cost 40,000 lives and the town of Cassino was destroyed.*

WWII IN ASIA AND THE PACIFIC

Timeline

During the 1930s, Japan expanded its influence in East Asia. That not only threatened Japan's neighbors, but it threatened American and British interests in the region. Japan joined the Axis in 1940, increasing the tensions between Japan, the United States, and Britain.

ATTACK ON PEARL HARBOR

On the morning of December 7, 1941, Japan launched a surprise attack on the American naval base at Pearl Harbor, Hawaii. Two waves of bombers struck the base, sinking or damaging 18 American ships and 292 airplanes, and killing or wounding more than 3,500 people. The damage could have been much worse, but much of the American fleet was out of the harbor on naval exercises at the time.

This attack shocked and angered the American people. Up to that point, they had been against joining the war. The United States declared war against Japan on December 8, 1941. Germany and Italy declared war on the United States a few days later. Hitler's greatest fear had come to pass: the United States and its mighty military had entered the war.

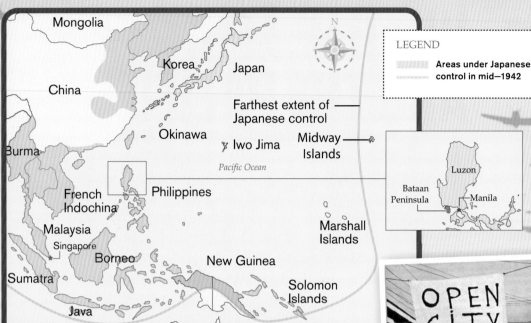

LEGEND

░░░░ Areas under Japanese control in mid—1942

ATTACK ON THE PHILIPPINES

The Japanese then focused on the Philippines, which was an American colony, defended by General Douglas MacArthur's troops. MacArthur planned to have his troops fall back into the heavily defended peninsula of Bataan on the island of Luzon. He believed they could hold the peninsula for six months while waiting for **reinforcements** to arrive. But it took only two weeks for the Japanese to take control.

The Battle for Bataan

On January 7, 1942, the Japanese laid siege to Bataan. MacArthur flew to Australia, and his command was handed to General Jonathan Wainwright. Wainwright wasn't told that the United States could not afford to send more troops to Bataan. The American and Filipino troops continued to fight but by the beginning of May, they had run out of supplies.

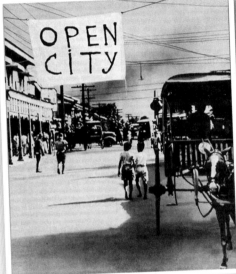

ABOVE: *On December 26, 1941, General MacArthur declared the Philippine capital, Manila, to be an open city.*

What Do You Know?

Bataan Death March

When the Japanese took Bataan, they captured thousands of American and Filipino soldiers. The Japanese forced the prisoners to march to the prison camps in San Fernando, 68 miles (110 km) north. The men were not given any food and only little water, despite the scorching heat. Between 6,000 and 11,000 men died during the six-day march.

THE BATTLE FOR SINGAPORE

While Japanese planes struck Pearl Harbor, additional forces were landing in Thailand and the Malay Peninsula in Malaysia. Japan wanted these areas for their natural resources, such as iron, aluminum, and oil. They also wanted to capture Singapore, which was a major city and important to British trade.

The British considered Singapore to be an undefeatable fortress. The city was extremely difficult to attack from the sea because the Royal Navy guarded it. The British also believed the thick Malayan jungle prevented an attack from the north. So the British were very surprised when the Japanese sank two of their most powerful warships, and Japanese troops approached on foot through the jungles north of the city.

Singapore fell quickly. The final blow came when bombing damaged the city's water source. On February 15, 1942, the British commander surrendered. It was a blow to British morale that it only took the Japanese 70 days to take the Malayan Peninsula.

LEFT and BELOW: *Fighting and moving troops through a jungle is difficult, particularly in sweltering heat. This is why the British did not expect an attack on Singapore from the north.*

BATTLES ON THE SEA

Things had not gone well for the Allies in the first months of the war in the Pacific, and they needed a victory to boost morale.

Battle of the Coral Sea

On May 4, 1942, a Japanese convoy was sailing to New Guinea. The U.S. Navy met the convoy in the Coral Sea, northeast of Australia. The two forces battled for four days, almost entirely from the air. The surface ships never saw one another. There was no clear winner, but the Japanese could not continue to New Guinea. That was enough to boost morale in the United States.

BELOW: *On June 19 and 20, 1944, the Japanese navy fought a much larger American force. This was the Battle of the Philippine Sea. The Japanese lost three carriers and about 600 aircraft.*

The United States Takes Control

By the middle of 1944, the Japanese seemed unable to stop the U.S. Navy. On October 23, 1944, Japan sent its largest naval force to attack American ships that were supporting the invasion of Leyte, in the Philippines. What followed was the Battle of the Leyte Gulf—the largest naval battle of the war. Japan lost so many ships and planes that the country didn't play a major role in the rest of the war.

ABOVE: *Japanese* kamikaze *pilots volunteered to sacrifice their lives by crashing explosives-filled planes into American ships.*

BATTLES ON LAND

As the United States made progress on the seas, their land forces began capturing Pacific islands held by the Japanese.

Guadalcanal

The first American land offensive came on Guadalcanal, which is one of the Solomon Islands. The Japanese wanted the island for controling the flow of supplies to Australia. The Americans wanted the island for launching attacks on Japan. The Japanese were building an airbase on the island, so on August 7, 1942, American soldiers stormed the island's beaches and captured the airfield.

The battle was costly: both sides lost ships and planes. But Japan suffered the most losses, particularly in the air. Finally, in February 1943, the Japanese were forced to retreat. This was a turning point because it signaled America's power at sea, in the air, and on the land.

Iwo Jima

On February 19, 1945, American marines landed on the beach of Iwo Jima, Japan. The U.S. Navy and Air Force had been pounding the island with artillery for days. The American soldiers did not know that about 21,000 Japanese soldiers were watching them from caves, tunnels, and dugouts on the island. Twenty minutes after the Americans landed, the Japanese opened fire.

ABOVE: *For six months, Japan and the United States fought for control of Guadalcanal.*

ABOVE: *By March 11, Iwo Jima was in American hands. The Japanese army, which would rather die than surrender, lost almost its entire 21,000-soldier force. Only 216 survived.*

ABOVE: *Fighting off the island of Okinawa*

surrender, American president Harry Truman decided to use the United States' new weapon—the atomic bomb. The first atomic bomb was dropped on Hiroshima on August 6, killing more than 80,000 people in seconds. The second atomic bomb was dropped on Nagasaki, killing 40,000 people.

After the second atomic bomb was dropped, Japan's Emperor Hirohito declared defeat, and Japan surrendered on August 15.

Okinawa

Okinawa was the last island the American forces had to take before attempting to take the Japanese mainland. As the Americans approached Okinawa, 100,000 Japanese soldiers waited for them in underground fortifications. Meanwhile, 2,000 *kamikaze* pilots crashed their planes into Allied ships. The fight was one of the fiercest of the war. More than 150,000 people died in the 11 weeks it took the United States to capture the island.

Tragedy in Japan

The American attacks on Japan were fierce. The bombing of Japanese cities between March and August 1945 are believed to have killed more than one million people. When Japan refused to

What Do You Know?

The bomb dropped on Hiroshima was nicknamed "Little Boy," though it was quite large. It had approximately the same explosive power as 15,000 tons (13,608 tonnes) of dynamite. "Fat Man," the bomb dropped on Nagasaki, had the same power as about 21,000 tons (19,051 tonnes) of dynamite.

BELOW: *On September 2, 1945, Japanese officials signed the terms of surrender aboard the USS* Missouri. *The war was over.*

FURTHER READING AND WEBSITES

BOOKS

Ambrose, Stephen E. *The Good Fight: How World War II Was Won.* Atheneum Books for Young Readers, 2001.

Harris, Nathaniel. *Timelines: World War II.* Arcturus Publishing, 2008.

Jeffrey, Gary. *Battle for the Atlantic.* Crabtree Publishing Company, 2016.

Jeffrey, Gary. *North Africa and the Mediterranean.* Crabtree Publishing Company, 2016.

Jeffrey, Gary. *The Eastern Front.* Crabtree Publishing Company, 2016.

Jeffrey, Gary. *The Secret War.* Crabtree Publishing Company, 2016.

Jeffrey, Gary. *The Western Front.* Crabtree Publishing Company, 2016.

Jeffrey, Gary. *War in the Pacific.* Crabtree Publishing Company, 2016.

Murray, Aaron R., ed. *World War II: Battles and Leaders.* DK Publishing, Inc., 2004.

Panchyk, Richard. *World War II for Kids.* Chicago Review Press, 2002.

Tonge, Neil. *Battles of World War II.* Rosen Publishing Group, 2009.

WEBSITES

World War II facts
kidskonnect.com/history/world-war-ii/

Interactive games and puzzles about WWII
www.nationalww2museum.org/see-hear/kids-corner.html

Veterans Affairs Canada's WWII website
www.veterans.gc.ca/eng/remembrance/history/second-world-war

Canada and the Second World War
www.warmuseum.ca/cwm/exhibitions/chrono/1931crisis_e.shtml

AUTHOR BIOGRAPHY

Kelly Cochrane has been an editor and technical writer for more than fifteen years. His background is in middle-school, high-school, and college education, with specialties in History and Communications. His work has taken him into diverse areas of study, but his primary focus is in the area of elementary and middle-school Social Studies and Geography, in particular the history, growth, and development of Canada as a country.

GLOSSARY

advance a movement forward into enemy territory

Allied forces (Allies) a group of countries that fought together during World War II, led by Britain, France, the Soviet Union, and the United States

ally a friend in a struggle or battle

artillery large weapons that fire large shells and are operated by a crew

Axis forces a group of countries that fought together during World War II, led by Germany, Italy, and Japan

Balkan Peninsula the countries in Europe's easternmost peninsula, which in 1939 included Yugoslavia, Albania, Bulgaria, Romania, Greece, and the part of Turkey on the European continent (today Yugoslavia has been broken into several countries, and Moldova is separate from Romania)

blockade a strategy of blocking the flow of supplies to an enemy, particularly at sea

bombarded struck something repeatedly with many blows, particularly with bombs or shells

charge an explosive device

civilians people who are not in the armed forces

colonies regions or countries that are controlled by other countries

convoy a group of ships that travel together and are escorted by warships or airplanes

dictator a ruler who controls a country with little to no input from the people

dilemma a situation in which all imagined actions lead to some kind of undesirable result

division a military unit of 10,000 to 20,000 troops

Dutch relating to the country of Netherlands

escort in military terms, relating to an armed force or weapon, such as a ship or plane, that travels with and protects an unarmed group

ferried carried across a stretch of water by boat

foothold a place that is securely held by a country or force, from which further attacks can be launched

fortification strongly built and defended location

front the line between two enemies fighting a war

heartland the center of a country, often where industry and agricultural riches exist

Holland a part of western Netherlands that was a province during World War II (it does not exist today), also the informal name of the country of Netherlands

intelligence in military terms, information gathered secretly then used to make plans

liberated set free

merchant sailors sailors on merchant ships

merchant ships supply ships that were not part of a navy and were usually unarmed (even though some had light weapons)

morale spirit and sense of hope

Nazi relating to a political party, led by Hitler after 1921, that believed in the unquestioned power of the government, expanding German territory, and discrimination against certain races, particularly Jewish people

neutral not involved and not supporting one side or the other

obstacle something that blocks the way

offensive in military terms, relating to major attacks

radar a technology that detects objects, such as planes and ships, by sending out radio waves through the air

rations a limited amount of goods, such as food and water given to each person or household

reinforcements more troops sent for added support

resistance the act of fighting back

sea mines explosive devices that either floated near the surface and exploded when they came in contact with a ship, or sat at the bottom of the sea and exploded when ships passed nearby

Siberia a region in northern Asia

sonar a technology used to locate objects by bouncing sound waves through the water

striking range the distance within which a weapon or a vehicle carrying a weapon, such as a plane, can deliver an attack or strike

terrain the land, including its geographical features (hills, valleys, mountains, rivers, vegetation, etc.)

torpedoes powerful explosive devices that travel through the water and strike a ship just below the waterline

wolf pack groups of U-boats that traveled together to attack surface ships

INDEX